TABLE OF CONTENTS

Player

MARCUS ALLEN

Born: March 26, 1960, at San Diego, California
Height: 6′2″
Weight: 205 lbs.
College: University of Southern California
High School: San Diego, California; Lincoln

The questions nagged Marcus Allen in the weeks before the 1982 National Football League draft. Here was a guy who had won the Heisman Trophy after setting a single-season college rushing record with 2,342 yards and who had rushed for 4,682 yards at USC.

Yet, the scouts wondered. Was he durable enough? Could he really be a feature back and take the rugged pounding of NFL football?

Said Dallas Cowboys personnel director Gil Brandt before the draft, "I just don't know if Marcus can carry a team. He is a back you can win with. But (O.J.) Simpson carried a team. (Tony) Dorsett can carry a team. I don't know if he can do that."

Six years later, Allen has rushed for more than 6,000 yards despite losing several games to two seasons because of player strikes. He has also caught more than 300 passes to display his versatility.

There is no question Allen carried his team during the 1985 season when he was named Player of the Year by The Sporting News. When injuries hit quarterbacks Jim Plunkett and Marc Wilson, the Raiders started giving Allen the ball more. And did he ever respond.

Allen carried 380 times for 1759 yards and added 67 receptions. His NFL rushing championship was the first ever for a Raiders running back. That season he set an NFL record for yards from scrimmage with 2,314 and he tied another mark by rushing for at least 100 yards in nine straight games.

Despite all the awards, Allen showed his team ethic by noting the Raiders' elimination from the playoffs by the New England Patriots.

Said Allen, "At the outset of each year, the measurement you use is going to the Super Bowl. While the awards are special, they're no consolation for not going to the Super Bowl."

The Super Bowl had been his showcase in Super Bowl XV. Against the Washington Redskins, Allen set a game record with 191 yards rushing and was named Most Valuable Player.

	Rushing Statistics				Receiving Statistics			
	Att.	Yards	Avg.	TDs.	No.	Yards	Avg.	TDs.
Career—6 Years	1,489	6,151	4.1	54	334	3,167	9.5	15

ROGER CRAIG

Born: July 10, 1960, at Preston, Mississippi
Height: 6′0″
Weight: 224 lbs.
College: University of Nebraska
Degree: Bachelor of Arts in Criminal Justice
High School: Davenport, Iowa; Central

To use the word versatile to describe San Francisco 49ers running back Roger Craig is almost redundant. Without much fanfare, Craig continues to be a consistent threat out of the 49ers' backfield—as a runner and receiver.

In 1985, Craig became the only player in National Football League history to pass 1,000 yards in one season in both rushing and receiving. He also set a league record for receptions by a running back with 92.

Sherman Lewis, San Francisco's running back's coach, once said of Craig, "If we featured Roger alone, he could gain 1,500 or 1,600 yards. Every year, he's gotten more comfortable with the offense, especially the running. He doesn't think anymore, he reacts, and it shows in the way he accelerates and takes off."

Ironically, Craig became adept at pass-catching despite having little experience in that area of the game in college. He caught just 16 passes during his college career and then-49ers assistant coach Paul Hackett said, "You had to scratch for even one shot of him as a receiver on film."

But the 49ers gambled with a second-round pick and it paid off. "He's just very special," said Coach Bill Walsh. "His dedication and drive are something to behold. He's a selfless, sacrificing athlete with great stamina. He's simply one of the great players in the league today."

And Craig has no problem with the way he's utilized in the 49ers' diversified offense. Talking about his role as a receiver, Craig said, "It makes sense what they do with me. It's really like a running play. Get me one-on-one with a linebacker and I know I'm going to win that battle."

Before his senior season in college, Craig moved to fullback to make way for Mike Rozier, who won the Heisman Trophy a year later. When asked to name the three most inspirational players during his time at Nebraska, Rozier named Craig.

	Rushing Statistics				**Receiving Statistics**			
	Att.	Yards	Avg.	TDs.	No.	Yards	Avg.	TDs.
Career—5 Years	964	4,069	4.2	34	358	3,234	9.0	14

ERIC DICKERSON

Born: September 2, 1960, at Sealy, Texas
Height: 6′3″
Weight: 220 lbs.
College: Southern Methodist University
High School: Sealy, Texas

Somehow, it just didn't fit. Here was running back Eric Dickerson, a guy everyone figured would wear a Los Angeles Rams uniform for the rest of his career, cavorting for the Colts, in Indianapolis of all places. And traded on Halloween to boot.

But it wasn't a dream or mirage. Dickerson had made himself unwelcome in Los Angeles because of constant contract demands and finally the Rams figured trading the best running back in the NFL would be addition by subtraction. So Dickerson was traded to Indianapolis, with the Colts sending unsigned linebacker Cornelius Bennett to the Buffalo Bills.

The Bills and Colts then sent a bushel of draft picks to the Rams, which they figured to use to rebuild the team. And Dickerson didn't miss a beat in Indianapolis. He fit right in and led the Colts to the division championship in the AFC East.

"I like it here, I really do," Dickerson said late in the 1987 season. But he admitted, "I'm surprised that I do. I know that's why the Rams sent me here, thinking I've gone to one of the worst outposts in the league. Some place that I'd hate.

"I didn't know anything about Indianapolis. Sure, there's not a whole lot to do here, but then I never did a whole lot. I never was L.A.-crazed. I miss some of my friends, but I don't miss L.A."

Clearly, merely the presence of Dickerson improved the Colts' attitude. Veterans suddenly figured management was serious about becoming a winner. And Dickerson blended in well.

Said Colts linebacker Johnie Cooks, "Eric is a positive player. Now, that may not sound right to those in Los Angeles, but Eric is a team player. What I like about him is that he's a regular person. He's making a lot of money, but it doesn't affect how he treats people. He's just a positive influence on the whole team the way he goes out and works as hard as anybody."

Dickerson wound up second in the NFL in rushing in 1987 with 1,288 yards and went over 8,000 yards in his career in his fifth season. It took Jim Brown 80 games to reach 8,000; Dickerson did it in 74. He has also rushed for at least 1,000 yards in five consecutive seasons.

But he's not content. Dickerson said he wants to play a total of 10 or 11 seasons before retiring. And if he maintains the pace of his first five years in the second five, Walter Payton's rushing record could be in jeopardy.

	Rushing Statistics				**Receiving Statistics**			
	Att.	Yards	Avg.	TDs.	No.	Yards	Avg.	TDs.
NFL Career— 5 Years	1,748	8,256	4.7	61	136	1,045	7.7	2

JOHN ELWAY

Born: June 28, 1960, at Port Angeles, Washington
Height: 6′3″
Weight: 210 lbs.
College: Stanford University
Degree: Bachelor of Arts in Economics
High School: Granada Hills, California

Denver Broncos quarterback John Elway has the distinction of leading a team to the Super Bowl two consecutive years. Unfortunately for Elway, both trips resulted in defeats. But that can't take away from the development he has shown after just five years in the National Football League.

Elway is truly the leader of the Broncos and his superior skills lifted Denver during the 1987 season when numerous injuries hit the offense. He was named NFL Most Valuable Player by the Associated Press and American Conference Player of the Year by three organizations.

Said Broncos Coach Dan Reeves, "John Elway unquestionably deserved all the honors that came his way last year. He truly was the most valuable player in the entire NFL, and it was great to see him recognized as such.

"When you have great quarterbacks, who have great arms, you are never out of a football game. John has tremendous confidence in his ability now because he has come through in so many tough situations to win games for us. Not only does he have confidence in himself, but John also has the confidence of our offensive and defensive units."

Elway has had to experience a lot and mature quickly since being the first player selected in the 1983 draft. Chosen by the then-Baltimore Colts, Elway didn't want to play for the Colts and was traded one week after the draft to the Broncos. But there were high expectations.

In one 1984 game, Elway threw five interceptions. His pregnant wife was at the game and a fan sitting near the players' wives yelled, "You can get your wife pregnant, but you can't do anything else." Janet Elway slapped the man.

Recalls Elway, "It was all part of growing pains. I guess fans are the same everywhere. Despite some rough times, I still think we've got the best in the world."

He had just better hope, though, that another Super Bowl loss isn't in the near future.

Passing Statistics

	Att.	Comp.	Pct.	Yards	TDs.	Int.
Career—5 Years	2,158	1,1680	54.1	14,835	85	77

JIM KELLY

Born: February 14, 1960, at Pittsburgh, Pennsylvania
Height: 6'3"
Weight: 218 lbs.
College: University of Miami
Degree: Bachelor of Science in Business Management
High School: East Brady, Pennsylvania

He has taken the city of Buffalo by storm. And to think, fans of the Bills wondered whether quarterback Jim Kelly would ever call Buffalo home. Drafted by the Bills in the first round of the 1983 draft, Kelly instead chose to sign with the Houston Gamblers of the United States Football League.

In the two seasons in the USFL, Kelly lit up the sky in the run-and-shoot offense made famous by Mouse Davis. In his first season with the Gamblers, Kelly threw 44 touchdown passes. But the style of offense also took its toll. He was sacked 110 times in two years, including 75 that first year. Kelly also rushed for 663 yards in two USFL seasons and scored six touchdowns.

But the USFL ceased operations in the summer of 1986 and Kelly's rights were still held by the Bills. Constant speculation had Buffalo trading his rights to another NFL team because it was perceived that he didn't care to play in Buffalo.

However, the Bills' front office was relentless in its pursuit of Kelly and he finally signed. Now he says the city is a perfect fit.

"I definitely feel good about my decision to play here," he said. "I'm proud to be a Buffalo Bill. In due time, when we bring this team around, people are going to start recognizing who the Buffalo Bills are. And there's not going to be a better place to be than Buffalo when that happens."

Kelly's toughness has helped the Bills and as he continues to learn NFL defenses, the greatness will come.

Said Bills quarterback coach Ted Marchibroda, "I don't know of anything we can't do with Jim. We're dealing with a guy who has the fewest limitations at that position since Bert Jones."

Even his opponents have become admirers. Said Cleveland Browns Owner Art Modell, "Jim Kelly is going to make people forget a lot of great quarterbacks. Once he learns how to read NFL defenses, he's going to be unstoppable."

Passing Statistics

	Att.	Comp.	Pct.	Yards	TDs.	Int.
NFL Career 2 Years	899	535	59.5	6,391	41	28
USFL Career— 2 Years	1,154	730	63.3	9,842	83	45

BERNIE KOSAR

Born: November 25, 1963, at Boardman, Ohio
Height: 6'5"
Weight: 210 lbs.
College: University of Miami
Degree: Bachelor of Arts in Finance and Economics
High School: Boardman, Ohio

Somehow it seems there is something out of place. Having already played three seasons in the National Football League and having led the Cleveland Browns to within one game of the Super Bowl in two consecutive seasons, when you look at the birthday, you figure there is a misprint.

It just can't be, right? A guy who plays with such poise and confidence but who will turn 25 during the 1988 season, his fourth in the NFL? But there is no mistake. Bernie Kosar, boy wonder, is that quarterback. And NFL opponents shudder to think he might only get better.

Said Browns Coach Marty Schottenheimer, "His progress on the field and in the classroom surpassed everyone's expectations. We knew we had a special person all along, but he captured everyone's confidence with his ability to win in any circumstance."

By all rights, Kosar should have been a rookie during the '87 season. But he entered the NFL after just three years at the University of Miami because he had earned his degree. While he attended class for three years, he played just two seasons.

He led Miami to a national championship and figured the time was ripe for pro football. He skipped the regular draft in 1985 and then petitioned for inclusion in a supplemental draft, a draft in which the Browns owned the first pick. When Cleveland realized Kosar might bypass the regular draft, the Browns acquired the first pick in any supplemental draft from Buffalo. The NFL now holds a lottery to determine the order of selection for supplemental drafts so no deals can be made before it takes place.

Kosar wanted Cleveland—he grew up 60 miles from Cleveland Stadium—and Cleveland wanted Kosar. The marriage is still in its honeymoon.

In 1987, Kosar led the Browns to their third straight AFC Central Division title and the team is 20-8 in his two full seasons as a starter. In that time frame, Kosar's interception ratio is a mere 2.0, the lowest in the NFL.

Passing Statistics

	Att.	Comp.	Pct.	Yards	TDs.	Int.
Career—3 Years	1,168	675	57.8	8,465	47	26

JIM McMAHON

Born: August 21, 1959, at Jersey City, New Jersey
Height: 6′1″
Weight: 190 lbs.
College: Brigham Young University
High School: Roy, Utah

He is the straw that stirs the Chicago Bears' drink. When quarterback Jim McMahon is healthy, it seems the Chicago Bears are almost unbeatable. The persona. The image. It all doesn't do justice to an actually quiet family man who knows how to do one thing best: win football games.

Unfortunately for the Bears, he spends too much time on the sideline with injuries thanks to his fearless play. In 1984, he missed two games. One because of a back injury and one because of a damaged kidney.

The following season he missed three games with a shoulder injury, but returned to lead the Bears to the Super Bowl and a dominating performance in a victory over the New England Patriots.

Troubles really set in in 1986. McMahon missed 10 games because of shoulder problems and eventually underwent surgery in December. Some said he might never play again. But McMahon was up to the task. He rehabilitated relentlessly in his effort to play again.

Said Bob Gajda, who worked closely with McMahon during his rehabilitation, "Jim is very disciplined personally. Not like his public image."

"People don't know that Jim will do whatever he has to do," said his agent Steve Zucker.

He made it back despite starting the season on injured reserve. After the strike he was ready. And the magic returned as McMahon became the starter again. A 25-game winning streak as the starting quarterback ended with a November 16, 31-29, loss to Denver, but that didn't end the McMahon mystique.

In fact, since becoming the Bears' No. 1 quarterback, the team is 41-14 in games he's started. Too bad about the games he couldn't start. It happened again at the end of the '87 season when he pulled a hamstring in a December 6 game against Minnesota. That meant another three games on the bench.

Said Coach Mike Ditka, when assessing the '88 season, "The main thing is for Jim to avoid injury. The off-season conditioning and the fact that he is over the shoulder injury will hopefully allow him to get in the kind of shape for him to come back and have an injury-free, successful season."

Passing Statistics

	Att.	Comp.	Pct.	Yards	TDs.	Int.
Career—6 Years	1,321	760	57.5	9,857	61	49

JOE MONTANA

Born: June 11, 1956, at Monongahela, Pennsylvania
Height: 6′2″
Weight: 195 lbs.
College: University of Notre Dame
Degree: Bachelor of Science in Business Administration
High School: Monongahela, Pennsylvania; Ringgold

San Francisco 49ers quarterback Joe Montana has had a career full of memories to fill his scrapbook. He has had record-breaking performances in several categories. He owns two Super Bowl rings as well as game Most Valuable Player trophies for each conquest.

But probably the thing he will always remember most when his playing days are over is the sock drill. During the 1986 season, doctors finally decided that for Montana to play football again, he would have to undergo back surgery. He had aggravated an old back injury in the first game of the season and a few days later, his left leg was growing numb.

After the surgery, it seemed doubtful that Montana would play again that season. But Montana would have none of that. An intensive rehabilitation program followed and was conducted by 49ers conditioning coach Jerry Attaway. Clearly at the bottom of Montana's list was that sock drill.

"The worst, the very worst," Montana would say later.

In the drill, Montana would go back as if to pass and Attaway would toss a weighted sock five to 15 yards to the right or left and Montana would run that way and set up to pass.

Said Attaway, "Next, I'd immediately pitch a sock the other way. And he'd twist, spin and race over there, and set up again. When his legs started to come back, I used three socks in a 10-minute drill, but that was about all. In 10 minutes of that, any well-conditioned quarterback would be almost worn out."

But it paid off. Montana played again that season and in 1987 threw a career-high 31 touchdown passes and also led all NFL quarterbacks with a passer rating of 102.1.

Concluded former 49ers tight end Russ Francis, "What you've seen of him over the years, well, a lot of it wasn't just ability. A lot of it was heart."

Passing Statistics

	Att.	Comp.	Pct.	Yards	TDs.	Int.
Career—9 Years	3,276	2,084	63.6	24,552	172	89

JERRY RICE

Born: October 13, 1962, at Starkville, Mississippi
Height: 6′2″
Weight: 200 lbs.
College: Mississippi Valley State University
High School: Crawford, Mississippi; Moor

Amazing statistics have always been a part of the arsenal of San Francisco 49ers wide receiver Jerry Rice.

In college, Rice set 18 NCAA Division I-AA records and totaled 4,693 receiving yards in his four seasons at Mississippi Valley state. In his final two collegiate seasons, Rice had more than 100 receptions each year and the numbers in his senior year were astounding: 1,845 yards and 28 touchdowns.

49ers scout Ernie Plank remembers a game he saw Rice play his senior season.

"He caught 12 passes and scored three touchdowns," Plank said. "In the first quarter. I thought I might see my first 40-receptions game."

By the end of the game, Rice had caught 17 passes for 294 yards and five touchdowns in an 86-0 win over Kentucky State.

His three-year pro career has also been filled with impressive performances. In 1986, Rice caught 86 passes for 1,570 yards and caught 15 touchdown passes. But that was merely a warmup for his record-shattering 1987 campaign.

Playing just 12 games because of the strike, Rice still caught 65 passes for 1,078 yards. Amazingly, of those 65 receptions, 22 were for touchdowns, an NFL record for one season. He also scored a touchdown on a rushing play for a league-leading 23 scores. Rice will also enter the '88 season with a record-breaking streak intact. He had caught touchdown passes in 13 consecutive games, dating back to the last regular season game of the 1986 season.

San Francisco Coach Bill Walsh proved to be something of a prophet during Rice's second season. Said Walsh, "We always have said that his best would come by his third or fourth year. But there is no better player at his position in the NFL right now. Some might be as good, but no one is better."

NFL defensive backs shudder to think that Rice's best will come his fourth season.

Receiving Statistics

	No.	Yards	Avg.	TDs.
Career—3 Years	200	3,575	17.9	40

HERSCHEL WALKER

Born: March 3, 1962, at Wrightsville, Georgia
Height: 6'1"
Weight: 225 lbs.
College: University of Georgia
High School: Wrightsville, Georgia; Johnson County

The torch has officially been passed in Dallas. It happened during the 1987 season. Cowboys Coach Tom Landry started the season believing he could find enough uses for Tony Dorsett and Herschel Walker playing at the same time.

What resulted was Walker playing a variety of positions, including wide receiver, but the club seemed to be missing a certain spark. It was a tough decision for Landry, but it was finally made: Dorsett went to the bench and Walker became the starting tailback. The move paid instant dividends.

In his first start, Walker rushed for 173 yards on 28 carries in a 23-17 overtime victory over New England on November 15. Sixty of those yards came on one run—a touchdown scamper in overtime that won the game. It was the longest overtime run from scrimmage in NFL history.

Walker started seven games at tailback during the '87 season and if his statistics for those games are projected over a normal 16-game season, it comes to over 1,500 yards rushing and 1,000 receiving.

On the final day of the season, Walker rushed for 137 yards and caught passes for another 50 against St. Louis. He became the first player in league history to gain more than 700 yards in both rushing and receiving in two different seasons. He also became the first Cowboys player to lead the team in rushing and receiving since Calvin Hill in 1973.

Looking to the future, Landry said of Walker, "We're counting on Herschel to play the dominant role because he has that kind of ability. We are building for the future with Herschel as the foundation. If he can stay healthy, we're going to be OK. Herschel is going to be singled out as the one guy you have to stop to beat the Cowboys."

The Cowboys got Walker's rights by gambling a fifth-round pick in the 1985 draft. Already playing in the United States Football League, Dallas figured he'd be available at some point. It came quicker than anticipated.

The USFL suspended operations in August, 1986, and Walker was quickly signed to a contract. And now 27 other NFL teams wonder how they could have failed to gamble a draft choice of their own in 1985.

	Rushing Statistics				Receiving Statistics			
	Att.	Yards	Avg.	TDs.	No.	Yards	Avg.	TDs.
USFL Career—3 Years	1,143	5,562	4.9	54	130	1,484	11.4	7
NFL Career—2 Years	360	1,628	4.5	19	136	1,552	11.4	3

CURT WARNER

Born: March 18, 1961, at Wyoming, West Virginia
Height: 5'11"
Weight: 205 lbs.
College: Pennsylvania State University
High School: Pineville, West Virginia

There have been many running backs to come through the National Football League with tremendous ability. But often, backs with great skills simply aren't able to withstand the pounding that comes constantly in NFL games.

Seattle Seahawks running back Curt Warner has proven he can not only take the hits but keep playing despite numerous aches and pains. It all began in 1984. Warner entered the NFL as the third player selected in the 1983 draft. He exploded on the scene with 1,449 yards and 13 touchdowns.

But disaster struck in the first game of the '84 season. Warner had already gained 40 yards on 10 carries against the Cleveland Browns when he tried to turn the right corner on a run. He planted and blew out his knee. It was an injury that has ended some players' careers, or at least kept some out for a full year.

However, Warner was ready for the start of the '85 season and despite being bothered by ankle spurs the entire season, he rushed for 1,094 yards. The ankle problems will probably always bother him and he has had frequent off-season surgery to relieve the problem.

In 1986, Warner rushed for 1,481 yards and followed that with 985 in the strike-affected 1987 season. The '87 campaign also brought nagging injuries. He banged up his ribs and shoulders before the strike. After the strike, he kept playing despite a turf toe injury that kept him out of practice. Then, an ankle was injured again in the third quarter of the final game of the season against Kansas City. That prevented him from reaching 1,000 yards rushing for the fourth consecutive season.

Still, he had played in 44 straight games since the 1984 knee injury.

Said Warner about playing with pain, "When the adrenaline goes, and you know you have to be out on the field, you take a lot more as far as pain tolerance than normal. An everyday type thing, I'm not geared up for. You pinch me, I'll get mad."

"You look at his face, and you don't know whether he's hurt or not, because all the time his face is squished up," said teammate John L. Williams. "When he's going to the huddle, the linemen ask me if he's all right, and I'll say he's fine. The more tired he gets, the better he plays."

	Rushing Statistics				Receiving Statistics			
	Att.	Yards	Avg.	TDs.	No.	Yards	Avg.	TDs.
Career—5 Years	1,189	5,049	4.2	42	148	1,160	7.8	4